YOUR KNOWLEDGE HAS

Vikas Rajole

Potential for Data Loss from Security Protected Smart-phones

Investigate how to use protective security measures from the PC world to secure Smartphones

GRIN Verlag

Bibliografische Information der Deutschen Nationalbibliothek:

Die Deutsche Bibliothek verzeichnet diese Publikation in der Deutschen National-
bibliografie; detaillierte bibliografische Daten sind im Internet über http://dnb.d-
nb.de/ abrufbar.

Imprint:

Copyright © 2011 GRIN Verlag GmbH
Druck und Bindung: Books on Demand GmbH, Norderstedt Germany
ISBN: 978-3-656-43789-5

This book at GRIN:

http://www.grin.com/en/e-book/214409/potential-for-data-loss-from-security-pro-
tected-smartphones

ROYAL HOLLOWAY, UNIVERISTY OF LONDON

Investigate how to use protective security measures from the PC world to secure Smartphones

Rajole Vikas

Submitted as part of the requirements for the award of the Msc in Information Security at Royal Holloway, University of London.

Acknowledgements

I would like to take this opportunity to thank the following persons for their input, help and support:

- My project supervisor at Royal Holloway: Dr Keith Mayes.
- Dr Chez Ciechanowic for his support throughout this MSc
- I would like to express my appreciation to all the professors at Royal Holloway who have increased my understanding of Information Security immensely over the course of the MSc, without which this project would not have been possible.
- Last, but not least, my parents and family for their kindness, support and encouragement.

Abstract

Smartphones have been widely accepted by mass market users and enterprise users. However, the threats related to Smartphones have also emerged. Smartphones carry substantial amount of sensitive data. There have been successful attacks in the wild on jail broken phones. Smartphones needs to be treated like a computer and has to be secured from all type of attacks.

There are proof of concept attacks on Apple iOS and Google Android. This project aims to analyse some attacks on Smartphones and possible solutions to defend the attacks. This project also uses a proof of concept malware for testing antivirus software.

Table of Contents

List of figures

List of Tables

Chapter 1
Introduction

1.1 Background

The way of communication and information exchange has changed rapidly over the past decade and yet it's a beginning of a new era of communication and information exchange. It started with Graham Bell's invention of the Telephone and it took about 140 years to drift from Graham Bell's Telephone system to Martin Cooper's Cell phone. Cell phones or mobile phones made people's life much easier than before. Mobile phones enabled voice and text communication on the go. However, since the release of iPhone in 2007, Smartphone has changed the way people communicate and exchange information. Smartphone is no more limited to voice and text messaging. With 3G mobile broadband and Wi-Fi access, Smartphone enables the use of internet on the go. Internet accounts such as email, Facebook, twitter and many more can be accessed using a Smartphone. Smartphone is accepted by enterprises for work as they believe that it increases employee productivity. Employees can access information required for work anywhere.

However, as technology evolves, the threats and risks associated to the Smartphone have also emerged. The use of internet on Smartphone requires protective measures like antivirus as used by a normal computer. A normal computer does not have to be directly internet facing. It can be in a private LAN and can access internet that is processed and protected by a firewall or an Intrusion Prevention System. A computer accessing Internet from a private LAN is less vulnerable to internet threats than the computers that are directly facing the internet. However, every Smartphone that uses mobile broad band is an internet facing device which makes it more vulnerable to internet related risks. The sales of Smartphone are growing exponentially and the threat landscape has also changed. Thus it has become vital to have the best protective measures to protect the Smartphone.

Chapter 2 analyses the components of computer and Smartphone antivirus for home users and enterprise users. It also compares some core components of some antivirus products.

Chapter 3 analyses some security features of Apple iOS and Google Android.

Chapter 4 uses a 'proof of concept' Smartphone malware to test against antivirus software.

Chapter 5 discusses the various attacks on Smartphones, the implications of the attack and possible protective measures against the attacks.

Chapter 6 analyses cloud based security solutions to protect Smartphones for enterprise users.

Below are some definitions that would help readers to understand the project.

Smartphone: It is a high end mobile phone that is capable of providing GPS navigation and internet access via mobile broadband and Wi-Fi access. It has a high resolution camera and touch screen with advanced computing capabilities. It can play multimedia files and display the standard web pages instead of the mobile optimized web pages. It allows access to most of the resources that are available on a computer like email, social networking and banking. It also allows to access company related work via enterprise developed applications.

Malware [1]: Malware is malicious software that can steal user sensitive data such as key strokes, browsing history, form data, credit card details, files, etc.

Trojan horse [2]: A Trojan horse is good looking software to disguise users that has a malicious software or code hidden in it that can steal data.

Root kit [3]: Root kit is malicious software that has System level privileges and kernel access of the machine and cannot be detected by antivirus software.

1.2 Project objectives

This project considers some of the threats to a Smartphone and discusses the possible protective measures. The project discusses about security solutions and security best practices for mass market users and enterprises. The project also discusses possible threats to a Smartphone, the source of the threat, the likelihood impact and protective measures. In the end, the project provides a brief summary and conclusion.

1.3 Methods used

The project considers various components of a computer antivirus and a Smartphone antivirus and compares the components to find conclusions. The project analyses the security features provided by Apple iOS and Google Android platforms. Understanding the security architecture of these platforms is important as it helps to find out the missing links to find effective security solutions. One major part of the project tests some trial version Smartphone antivirus products against a *'Proof of Concept'* malware on a phone with root access. The project analyses various antivirus products available to secure Smartphones. To analyse various antivirus products, the project refers to the technical information available on the website of the antivirus vendor. Whitepapers are also referred for additional information. The next chapter discusses the various components of a computer and Smartphone antivirus.

Chapter 2 Understanding the Antivirus Application

2.1 Introduction

Definition of Antivirus [4]: It is software that checks for malicious code based on signatures or behaviour of the malicious code.

It is important to understand how the antivirus software for computer and antivirus software for Smartphone works. This will help to analyse if a particular feature that is available in computer antivirus software could be included to enhance security of Smartphone. This chapter discusses the components of a computer antivirus and Smartphone antivirus for mass market and enterprise users.

2.2 Components of a conventional or computer Antivirus

Conventional antivirus software used on PC and Laptops can be categorized on the type of users.

1. **Home users:** The antivirus software for home users or mass market users usually contains features concentrating on internet security. The antivirus software for home users combines the Antivirus, Antispyware and Internet security features. Norton also includes Backup feature in the antivirus software. The internet security feature usually checks for malicious websites. The antivirus vendors update the malicious website database regularly. The home user antivirus combines these features in one product so that users get multiple security features in one product.

2. **Enterprise users:** The Enterprise antivirus has the antivirus and antispyware features and additional features such as Application and device control, Host Integrity, System lock down, Application White listing and black listing, Network access control, etc. Usually enterprises have a proxy firewall to filter web traffic at the network level to reduce the load on the end computers. Enterprise antivirus is capable of allowing or blocking applications, allowing or blocking removable devices. As per the organization policy, organizations might want to restrict use of certain applications. In some instances of research or software development, computers are locked down to allow only certain application due to strict development or research environment. Even updates might not be allowed to be installed once the system is

locked down. Enterprises have their own backup strategy so the backup is not coupled with the antivirus product.

Below are some of the components of conventional antivirus product used on computers

- **Antivirus and Antispyware Protection** [5]: It identifies and mitigates the threats that try to or have gained access to the computer by using the signatures. It looks for Virus, Trojan, Spyware, Adware, Key loggers, worms, and root kits. This feature also provides protection for email attachments.

- **Proactive or Real Time Threat Protection** [6]: It provides zero day protection for unknown threats based on anomaly. A threat might not get detected by the antivirus or antispyware feature if the product does not have the signature for the threat. Proactive scan has a process running at all times which looks for suspicious behaviour like key loggers, password stealers, etc.

- **Intrusion Prevention System** [7]: The intrusion detection engine uses deep packet inspection to check for port scans and denial-of-service attacks and protects against known buffer overflow attacks. Intrusion Prevention System also supports the automatic blocking of malicious traffic from infected computers to prevent further infection of computers in the network. Based on the Intrusion Prevention System alert information, administrators can review the logs and patch the systems to prevent intrusions and vulnerability exploits.

- **Firewall** [8]: The firewall contains the rules to allow or block traffic based on IP address, ports applications, services, protocol (e.g. TCP, UDP, ICMP, etc.), and direction (inbound or outbound) to allow or block traffic.

Some products offer additional features such as-

- **Host Integrity** [9]: It is a component that checks a host's integrity that attempts to connect to a network based on the Host Integrity rules. A Host Integrity rule defines the required software and the version or patches a host should have before it connects to the network. If the host does not fulfil the host integrity policy requirements, it is assigned an IP address of quarantine VLAN (Virtual Local Area Network) and is flagged to the administrator's attention to install the required software and patches.

12

- **System Lock Down** [10]: It is a feature that allows the administrators to restrict the files that can be executed on a computer. Administrators create an image of the operating system with a set of programs that are allowed to execute on the computer. A list of hash values of these programs is created and provided to the antivirus software that monitors all the programs. Any program whose hash value is not present in the list is not allowed to execute.

- **Application white listing and black listing** [11]: Administrators can add an application to the white list, so that antivirus does not detect programs that look like malicious to the antivirus software. There are some malicious applications like screenshot capturing tools that administrators use for monitoring. Even if the application is legitimate, administrators can black list applications if the use of application is not permitted by corporate policies.

- **Application and device control:** This feature allows the administrator to block applications based on hash vales from execution without having to do a complete lockdown. Device control is a feature that allows that allows blocking or allowing devices based on device class or can get even granular to block only a specific device of a particular class.

- **Network Access control** [12]: It allows controlling the network access of devices based on the IP address or the software running on the computer. Network Access control is usually used with Host Integrity to control network access at host or operating system level.

- **Proactive removable device scanning:** The antivirus software proactively displays a notification to the user to scan a removable devise such as USB pen drive whenever it is connected.

The table below compares some key features of a computer antivirus for some popular home user antivirus products.

Features	Norton [13]	McAfee [14]	Kaspersky [15]	Webroot [16]
Antivirus & Antispyware	Yes	Yes	Yes	Yes
E mail protection	Yes	Yes	No	No
Proactive threat protection	Yes	Yes	Yes	Yes
Firewall	Yes	Yes	Yes	No
Internet security	Yes	Yes	Yes	No
Pc tune-up	Yes	Yes	Yes	Yes
Online and offline Backup	Yes	Yes	No	Yes
Parental controls	No	Yes	Yes	No
Identity Protection	Yes	No	Yes	Yes

Table 1 Comparison of features of computer antivirus products for home users

2.3 Components of a Smartphone antivirus

Smartphone antivirus has lesser components as compared to computer antivirus. One reason could be the operating system architecture of the Smartphone. Android and iOS are designed with security in mind so that users don't have to rely too much on third party software's for security. Computer antivirus concentrates more on malware, Trojan and Internet security. Smartphone's antivirus application concentrates on features like - call/text blocking, Antitheft, parental control and Backup.

14

Below are some of the components of a typical Smartphone Antivirus.

- **Antivirus:** This component scans for known threats like, Malware, Trojan malicious code.

- **Firewall:** Monitors web traffic and filters malicious web pages.

- **Antitheft** [17]: This feature enables to get the phone location in case it is lost or stolen, using the GPS feature of the phone. It gives the GPS location of the device to the user which helps the user to track the phone. User can configure an action after maximum failed login attempts. The phone can be configured to reset itself to factory settings and wipe personal data like contacts, application settings, files from SD card. The phone can also be configured to lock itself if the SIM card is changed.

- **Parental control** [18]: This feature allows parents to monitor and block SMS or calls to unwanted numbers.

- **Backup** [19]: This feature allows to backup contacts and other data to the web, it also allows restoring data to new phones.

- **Call/text Blocking** [20]: A user can configure the antivirus to block phone calls like telemarketing and spam SMS messages from certain unwanted numbers.

- **Application Audit** [21]: This feature is not found in many Smartphone antivirus products. It monitors activity of all the applications and maintains a list of the permissions the application has, it also maintains the details of the applications that can send sensitive data and could charge bill to the user for its services.

The below table shows a comparison of features for some products-

Product	Antivirus	Web Security	Anti-Theft	GPS Tracking	Parental Control	Backup	App Auditing
Norton Mobile Security [22]	Yes	Yes	Yes	Yes	No	No	No
Kaspersky Mobile Security [23]	Yes	Yes	Yes	Yes	Yes	No	No
Webroot For mobile [24]	Yes	Yes	Yes	Yes	No	No	Yes
MaCafee Mobile Security [25]	Yes	Yes	Yes	Yes	No	Yes	No
Bitdefender Mobile Security [26]	Yes	Yes	Yes	Yes	No	No	Yes
BullGuard Mobile Security [27]	Yes	Yes	Yes	Yes	Yes	Yes	No
Trend Micro Security for Android [28]	Yes	Yes	Yes	Yes	No	No	Yes
Lookout Mobile Security [29]	Yes	Yes	Yes	Yes	No	Yes	No

Table 2 Comparison of features of Smartphone antivirus for home users

2.4 Comparison of computer antivirus and Smartphone antivirus

While computer antivirus provide a wide array of security features, Smartphone antivirus have limited features. One reason could be the limited computing capabilities of the Smartphone as compared to computers and the battery life. If a Smartphone antivirus has too many features, clearly it would use too many resources and it could slow down the Smartphone which could result in bad end user experience. Thus, it is up to the end user to decide what kind of security features they are looking for and then choose a best antivirus that suite their needs.

Computer antivirus mainly focus on threats like Virus, Malware, Trojans, Spyware, Key loggers, Root kits, Zero day attacks, Intrusion Prevention, Firewall and Internet security. As Smartphones are designed with security in mind, most of the Smartphone antiviruses don't have to worry about features like Malware, Spyware, key loggers, root kits, intrusion prevention. Smartphone antivirus mainly concentrates on security of the device in case the device is lost or stolen. Smartphone antivirus concentrates on features like Anti-theft, GPS tracking and Remote wipe. There two features that are not found in most of the antivirus software is 'Backup' and 'Application Auditing'.

2.5 Smartphone Security for enterprises

Many enterprises have accepted Smartphones to be used by employees to allow mobile access to corporate resources as organisations believe it increases in employee productivity. While Smartphones increase business productivity, businesses should also consider the risks associated to it. The reason is quite simple; there has been a rise in the number of attacks against Smartphones. Moreover, there are multiple platforms for Smartphones namely, Windows 7 mobile, iOS, Android, Symbian, Blackberry and HP web OS. Blackberry is designed for enterprise customer in mind whereas other phones are designed for multimedia and mass market customers in mind. Thus enterprises should treat Smartphones as corporate assets and include it under the umbrella of corporate policies. Enterprises must design an acceptable corporate usage policy for Smartphones. Enterprises should decide whether the employees could use their personal phone for work. Enterprises should create employee awareness regarding Smartphone usage and employees should be aware of the corporate Smartphone usage policies.

Below are some key points to improve Smartphone security for enterprises [30].

a. Ensure password is configured to access the phone. Password policy should be simple so that it is easy for users to remember the password or else users might write the password on a paper.

b. Administrators should configure device remote wipe after certain attempts of failed logins.

c. Encrypt removable SD cards to prevent loss of data in case the phone is lost or stolen.

d. Configure the device to lock after certain time of inactivity (for example 30 seconds)

e. Prohibit jail broken phones from accessing enterprise networks.

f. Ensure the phone meets minimum requirements of software versions before it connects to the enterprise network.

g. Use host integrity and network access control for Smartphones before they connect to enterprise networks.

h. Encrypt corporate data that resides on the phone and limit the amount of data that could be stored on the phone.

i. Ensure Smartphones have Antivirus and firewall software installed.

j. Filter and log inbound and outbound traffic of the phones.

k. Irrespective of what platform the Smartphone uses ensure it has the latest firmware.

l. Quarantine compromised device to stop further infection.

m. Ensure that the device is wiped securely at the 'end of life' before it is disposed.

n. Use Smartphone management software to manage the Smartphones to enforce corporate policies are enforced to the devices.

Like there are specially designed computer antivirus products for home and enterprise users similarly, there are Smartphone antivirus products for mass market and enterprise customers. 'Enterprise Mobile Management' software provides a centralized management platform to manage all the Smartphones and enforce corporate security policies to all the devices. Below are some of the enterprise antivirus products.

Symantec: Symantec provides an array of mobile management solutions for Smartphones. Symantec's *"Endpoint Protection Mobile Edition"* provides centralized management of mobile phones for Windows Mobile and Symbian. It can also include *"Network Access Control Mobile Edition"* to enforce Host integrity and network access control. The two products, *"Endpoint Protection Mobile Edition"* and *"Network Access Control Mobile Edition"* can be combined together. Symantec's *"Mobile Encryption powered by PGP"* allows encrypting email and other data on the phones.

Kaspersky: *'Kaspersky Endpoint Security for Smartphone'* supports four mobile platforms; Android, Blackberry, Windows Mobile and Symbian. It provides all the features available in a mass market antivirus for Smartphone with encryption as an additional feature for enterprise customers. While Kaspersky supports four mobile platforms, it does not provide host integrity and network access control.

McAfee: *"McAfee Enterprise Mobility Management"* supports all the four major mobile platforms iOS, Android, Windows Mobile and HP webOS. Like Kaspersky and Symantec, It provides all the features available in a mass market antivirus for Smartphone however, it does not provide encryption. On the other hand *'McAfee Enterprise Mobility Management'* provides host integrity and network access control.

Product	Encryption	Host Integrity & NAC	Android	iOS	Windows Mobile	Symbian	HP webOS
Symantec [31]	Yes	Yes	No	No	Yes	Yes	No
Kaspersky [32]	Yes	No	Yes	No	Yes	Yes	No
McAfee [33]	No	Yes	Yes	Yes	Yes	No	Yes

Table 3 Summary of the key features of some enterprise antivirus products

The next chapter will discuss the various security features provided by Apple iOS and Google Android platforms.

19

Chapter 3 An overview of iOS and Android security features

3.1 Introduction

In my opinion, iOS and Android architecture provides good security features as compared to security provided by computer operating systems like windows and Linux. iOS and Android provide good security features so that users don't have to rely too much on third party software for security. This chapter will analyse five security features which are- Traditional access control, Application provenance, encryption, isolation or sandboxing and permission based access control. These security features are described in Symantec's Whitepaper [34]. The implementation of the five security features varies for Android and iOS. This chapter analyses the security features provided by iOS and Android and some exploits.

3.2 Security features of Apple iOS

Apple iPhone's iOS is based on Apple's Mac OSX.

I. **Access control:** iOS provides traditional access control mechanism to login to the device. Administrators can configure the strength of the password and the frequency at which the password has to be changed. Administrators can also configure to wipe the device after a certain attempts of failed login.

II. **Digital signing of applications:** Any application that has to be executed on iOS has to be digitally signed. Apple has a strict digital signing process. Any developer who wishes to publish an application for iOS has to go through a signing process which includes paying an annual licensing fee. The developer has to digitally sign the application which attaches the developer's identity with the application. The digital signing of an application proves that the application is developed by Apple approved developer.

There are two ways of digitally signing an application for iOS.

A. **Individual:** Any individual developer who wishes to publish the application to Apple's app store must first submit the application to Apple for certification. Apple takes one to two weeks to complete the certification of the submitted application. Once the certification is completed, the application is published on Apple's app store for the users.

20

B. **Enterprise:** Any enterprise that wishes to develop a proprietary in house app for their internal organizational use must register the *'iOS Developer Enterprise Program'* [35]. The apps developed by the organization can be installed on the devices that have the organizations digital certificate. Apple prohibits sale of in house apps to third parties. Apple would revoke the organization's participation in the *'iOS Developer Enterprise Program'*.

The digital signing of applications is effective to block malware because of the following reasons-

A. Application development for iOS requires a signing process. This keeps the malware writers away from malicious app development because they will be prosecuted if they are caught.

B. Apple goes through a rigorous testing of the application before it is published.

C. Once the app is published, Apple's signing model prevents from tampering the application.

Windows 8 for computers will be introducing application signing to be more immune to virus and malware.

III. **Encryption:** Apple provides two level encryption to protect the data in an event if, the phone is lost or stolen. The first level encrypts the data in the flash memory with AES 256. The second level encrypts other data like email. A copy of the secondary encryption is in the memory as the iOS will need to allow background applications to read and write data. The iOS encrypts some part of the data in such a way that it is accessible only if the device is unlocked by typing the user password. The entire device, including the ROM and the SD card is encrypted. So in other words, in order to wipe the device, the key can be destroyed if the device is lost or stolen. Administrators can configure the device to wipe after a certain failed login attempts.

However, a German research institute Fraunhofer, demonstrated a highly sophisticated attack to bypass the hardware encryption process on an updated locked iPhone iOS running 4.2.1. However, this is beyond the skills of a normal attacker.

IV.   **Isolating processes or Sandboxing:** The iOS sandboxing isolates each application from other applications in such a way that, every application has an impression that it is the only application running on the device. Apps cannot view or modify data of other apps and even cannot find out the names of other installed apps. Apps cannot install privileged drivers or cannot gain administrator level access to the device. Apps are also isolated from user data such as contacts and emails. The benefit of isolation is that, even if an app is compromised, it cannot affect or further compromise other apps. This effectively stops the spread of malware to other apps unlike the malware in computer. However, an infected app like Safari web browser could execute malicious code and steal user sensitive data such as browsing history, passwords and credit card details. Thus the isolation process prevents a malware from infecting other apps and prevents installing kernel level drivers.

V.   **Permission based access control:** There are only four iOS system services to which an app may request access permission. Rest all services are explicitly allowed or blocked. The services are-

- Access to Global Positioning System (GPS) data.

- Receive notification from cloud based internet services for the apps running on the device.

- App may request permission to initiate an outgoing call.

- App may request permission to send SMS or email.

The user will be notified by iOS if an app tries to access any of these features. For the GPS data and the cloud based internet service, the user is asked for access permission once. Once the user grants the permission, the user is not prompted for the subsequent accesses. However, for the outgoing calls, SMS and email, the user intervention is required. This is to avoid spam SMS messages to premium numbers and spam emails.

Exploits on iOS: There have been no known attacks in the wild for non-jail broken phones. There have been exploits for jail broken iPhones. Ashley Towns from Australia wrote a worm for jail broken iPhone called 'ikee' [36]. The worm scanned for IP ranges which belonged to operators that sold iPhone. Whenever the worm found an iPhone it checked if SSH port 22 is open and tried to login as root with the default password "alpine". Once the worm gets root access, it changed the wallpaper to Rick Astley. There was another similar kind of worm that locked the phone and changed the wallpaper that displayed a message to pay 5 Euros to the hacker's PayPal account. In another phishing attack for jail broken iPhones in Netherland, the worm changed the etc. file. The etc file was changed to redirect the traffic going to mijn.ing.nl to a hacked IP 210.233.73.206 which is a pottery site in Tokyo. Mijn.ing.nl is the website for a famous European bank ING. The webpage at IP 210.233.73.206 had exact replica of the ING bank's login page to steal user credentials [37].

3.3 Security features of Google Android

Android uses non-standard Java platform called Dalvik and Linux. Programs are written in Java and then compiled using Google tools. Android is open source, which makes it open for security scrutiny by experts. One reason why Android has less vulnerability is because of its openness which allows security experts to scrutinize the code for security flaws.

I. **Access control:** Android's access control is similar to iPhone. It can be configured for maximum number of login attempts, wipe the device after certain login attempts and password strength. Android allows administrators to configure how often the login password should be changed.

II. **Digital signing of applications:** Application signing for Android is not rigorous as Apple. Anyone who wishes to develop an application for Android does not have to obtain certificate from Google, they can create their own certificate, develop an application and publish it in the Android market. A malicious developer can create a certificate by providing fake information. This is one reason why there are more malwares and Trojans for Android. Unlike Apple, Android does not verify the application before it is published. Android checks the application when it is reported to be malicious and removes it from Android market once it confirms it. Developers have to pay $25 to Google using a credit card, the credit card details is only the way to associate a developer to an app. However, a malicious developer might use someone else's credit card to save their identity. Android also allows users to download and install apps from internet and external SD card.

III. **Encryption:** Android introduced Encryption which uses AES 128 with CBC for tablets from Android 3.2 which is also called as Honeycomb [38]. It is a Kernel level implementation. However, Android for Smartphone's does not support encryption. This is a potential risk as anyone with physical access to the device can read the data from the memory card bypassing the access control mechanism.

IV. **Isolating processes or Sandboxing:** While applications for Android are written in Java, Android does not rely on Java's sandbox feature to isolate applications it has its own application isolation policy. Android implements a stringent isolation policy in such a way that no application is allowed get administrator or kernel level access. Every application runs in its own sandbox and has the rights that it is allowed. An application cannot access data of

24

another application however; an application might invoke another application. For example, when a user accessing email using the email application clicks on a web link, the email application invokes the web browser application. If a malware exploits a vulnerability of an application, the attack is limited to the application. A malware cannot affect other applications or nor can it get administrator or kernel access thus blocking the malware from infecting other applications. However, if an application like a web browser is exploited by malicious code, it can steal information such as browsing history, form data like password and credit card details, etc.

V. **Permission based access control:** Android implements a strict permission based access control policy for applications. An application cannot be installed silently with user notification. User interaction is required to install any kind of application which prevents a lot of 'drive by download' attacks. Android maintains a list of permissions an app is requesting. It displays the access permissions requested by an app to the user, if the user chooses to agree and install, the app is installed. If the user wishes to abort the installation, the application is not installed.

Chapter 4 Testing 'Proof of Concept' Smartphone malware against antivirus software

4.1 Introduction

This chapter tests a Proof of Concept malware against a few trial version Smartphone antivirus products. The 'Proof of Concept' malware if developed by Georgia Weidman. There are two versions of the proof of concept malware which are available for download from Georgia's website. The first version of the malware swallows the SMS messages sent to the infected phone. In other words the malware deletes the SMS once it hits the modem of the phone. The SMS is not sent to the application layer that displays the message to the end user. Another version of the malware is capable of reading the SMS and detecting if it has to send a spam to a specified number without user intervention. This project uses the first version of the malware for testing the malicious activity by the malware. The testing is aimed to find out whether an antivirus detects this activity by the malware. The malware is specifically designed for T-Mobile HTC G1 and it works on phones that have root access. Another reason to choose HTC G1 is the cost factor. The phone was purchased from eBay for £65, where as an iPhone is costlier, ranging in between £300 to £500 pounds.

4.2 The testing process

The three steps of the testing process are-

1. **Rooting Android for HTC G1**
2. **Running the BOT application as root**
3. **Testing the Antivirus**

Prerequisites:

A T-Mobile HTC G1 with root access is required to perform the testing.

4.2.1 Rooting Android for HTC G1

In real world, applications other than the operating system components and kernel don't have root access to the Smartphone operating system, unless vulnerability is exploited. This part of the chapter refers two YouTube videos [39] [40] to get root access on the mobile phone. The references of the rooting process and the files used in the rooting process are mentioned in the references section. A brief overview of the rooting process is as follows-

a. **The details of the HTC G1 Android before rooting are-**
Firm ware version: 1.6
Base band version: 62.50s.20.17u_2.22.19.261
Kernel version: 2.6.29-00479-g3c7df37 andriod-build@apa26#19
Build number: DRC92

b. **Downgrade firmware to version 1.0:** Download the RC7 [41] ROM for UK which is the official 1.0 Android ROM for G1.
Extract the *'DREAIMG.NBH'* file, copy it to the root of the SD card and turn off the phone. Boot the phone in recovery mode by pressing the Power + Home keys. The phone displays a triangle with exclamation mark, press *'Alt + L'*. Reset the phone to factory settings, to do this select *'Wipe data/factory reset option'* by following the on screen instructions. Power-off the phone by plugging out the battery. Plug in the battery and press the Power + camera button which brings up the boot loader screen. The boot loader automatically checks for the *'DREAIMG.NBH'* file and starts loading it. Follow the instructions to update the image to the phone. To reboot the phone, press the menu, call and power keys all at the same time.

c. **Update the firmware version manually from 1.0 to 1.5:** Once the phone is up and running, connect the USB cable and delete the *'DREAIMG.NBH'* file from the SD card. Download the file *'signed-kila-ota-148830.de6a94ca.zip* [42]*'*, rename it to update.zip and copy it to the root of the SD card and turn off the phone. Power on the phone by pressing the Home + Power keys together. Press Alt + L to see a list of options. Select the 'apply sdcard:update.zip' option by pressing Alt + s. Press the Home + Back keys together to reboot. At this point, the phone has firmware version 1.5, build CRB43.

d. **Configure Android to allow installation from unknown sources:** Got to Menu > Settings > Applications > select Unknown Source and click Ok.

e. **Flash Custom recovery image:** Download the files 'flashrec.apk [43]' and 'recovery-RA-dream-v1.5.2.img [44]' and copy them to the SD card. Using the 'Market', search and install file manager application like ASTRO file manager. Open the file manager application and browse the SD card contents to install the *'flashrec'* application from the

27

SD card. Open flashrec, it allows flashing a custom recovery. Select the 'Backup recovery Image' option by using the track ball or by tapping it. Once it says 'Backed up', type the name of the custom image file */sdcard/recovery-RA-dream-v1.5.2.img* and select 'Flash custom recovery image'. Once it displays 'Flashed new recovery image', power-off the phone.

f. **Install SPL which allows installing custom ROM:** Press the Power + Home key to boot in custom recover mode. Meanwhile on the computer, download *haykuro_new_spl-signed.zip* [45]. To copy the downloaded file to the SD card of the phone, connect the phone to the computer using a USB cable and on the phone select 'USB-MS Toggle'. Once the file is copied to the SD card, Press 'Home' key to disable USB access and unplug the USB cable. Select the option 'Flash zip from sdcard' and then select the *'haykuro_new_spl-signed.zip'* file. Follow the instructions to complete the installation.

g. **Partition the SD card:** Next step is to partition the SD card, to do this, select 'Partition sdcard'. Follow the onscreen instructions to create a 'Swap' partition of 96 MB, 512 MB for EXT2 and the rest for FAT32. Convert the newly created ext2 partition to ext3, to do this, select the 'SD: ext2 to ext3' option to convert.

h. **Install the custom ROM Cyanogen which allows root access:** Download the files 'signed-dream_devphone_userdebug-ota-14721.zip [46]' and 'update-cm-4.2.13-signed.zip [47]'. On the phone, enable 'USB-MS toggle' once again and copy both the files to the phone by using the USB cable. Disable USB by pressing Home key once the files are copied and unplug the USB cable from the phone. To install the zip files, select the option *'Flash zip from sdcard'*. The phone displays the names of the two zip files that were copied. First select the 'signed-dream_devphone_userdebug-ota-14721.zip'. Once it is installed, select the 'update-cm-4.2.13-signed.zip' to install. Press the Home + Back keys to complete the installation and reboot the phone. The phone now has Cyanogen with root access. It has a terminal emulator to get root access. The firmware details of the phone are as below-

        Firmware Version: 1.6

        Build Number: DRC83

        Mod version: CyanogenMod - 4.2.13.

        Kernel Version: 2.6.29.6-cm42 shade@toxygene

4.2.2 Running the BOT application as root

The 'Proof of Concept' BOT is developed by Georgia Weidman. A precompiled BOT application that swallows the SMS is available on her website [48]. Georgia has also presented a webinar at BrightTalk webinars on SMS Botnets [49]. She has also provided the source code for a BOT that is capable of reading SMS and sending SPAM SMS to the specified number. However for testing purpose, the precompiled 'safebot' application will be used. Once the phone is rooted, copy the precompiled 'safebot' file to the SD card that is available on the website. Follow the below instructions to run the Proof of Concept 'safebot' application.

a. The phone is now running Cyanogen which comes with a terminal emulator. Open the terminal emulator and type 'su root' to get super user or root access.

b. Android would display a kind of Microsoft Windows style 'User Access control' pop-up like the one displayed below. Select remember and click 'Allow'

Figure 1 Terminal window requesting access as root user

c. Close the terminal window and open it again. Type 'su root' once again, this time the prompt should change from '$' to '#'

d. Move the safebot file from sdcard to 'data' folder, by using the below commands.

#cd sdcard

#cp safebot ../data

29

e. As suggested by Georgia, rename the 'smd0' folder to 'smd0real' that's in the 'dev' folder. To do this type the below commands-

#cd ../dev

#mv smd0 smd0real

f. Give 'read', 'write' and 'execute' permission to 'safebot' and then run it by using the below commands-

#chmod 777 safebot

#./safebot

g. At this stage, the phone might freeze or might seem like nothing is happening. The phone did freeze and restart occasionally after running the safebot application. Press the 'Menu' key and select 'Reset term' option as displayed in the below image.

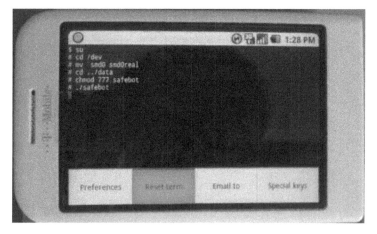

Figure 2 reset terminal window to go back to the prompt

h. The 'Reset term' option resets the terminal window and return to the '$' prompt. However, the safebot application will still be running. This can be verified by typing the below command-

#ps | grep safebot

30

i. Once the safebot application is running, the radio application needs to be killed as suggested by Georgia on her website. Type 'su root' to get root access once again to find the process id of the radio application and kill it by using the below commands-

#ps | grep rild

This command will display the process id for the radio application, for example 123. To kill the radio application, type the following command.

#kill 123

j. At this stage the safebot application is running as 'root' as displayed in the below image.

Figure 3 'safebot' application is running as 'root'

31

4.2.3 Testing the Smartphone Antivirus

Before running the safebot application as root, send a SMS to the phone to verify it receives the SMS. Once you confirm that the phone receives the SMS, start the safebot application as root by following the above steps. Send another SMS to verify that the safebot application swallows the SMS and does not display it to the user. If the above steps are done correctly, the SMS will be swallowed by the safebot application. For testing purposes two Antivirus software for Smartphones are used which are, 'Norton for Mobile Security Lite' and 'MaCafee mobile Security' that is available for free at Android market. The following steps are followed to test both the Antivirus software.

a. Install the antivirus software and restart the phone (though it is not required)

b. Confirm that the antivirus software is running by running the 'ps' command in the terminal window. The below image shows the antivirus process is running.

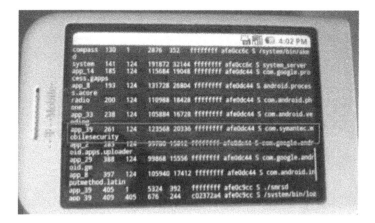

Figure 4 Symantec mobile security is running as an application

c. Start the safebot application as mentioned in step 2.

d. Send a SMS to check whether the antivirus detects or displays a notification of the malicious activity by the safebot application.

4.3 Test results

The proof of concept malware 'safebot' application is used for testing purposes to detect whether the activities of an application running as root are detected by an antivirus application. Clearly, an application that swallows SMS messages that are intended for the user is a malicious activity.

There are some legitimate applications that send SMS messages on behalf of the user. However, the 'End User License Agreement' states the fact that the application might send SMS messages to which the user has to accept if he or she wishes to install the application. Once the user accepts the 'End User License Agreement' and installs the application, the application might send SMS for intended purposes. The Smartphone operating system also displays a 'User Access Control' style window that says "The following application intends to send SMS message, do you want to allow". This could be a onetime permission request action for an application. It is justified for an application to send SMS without user intervention under certain conditions where the user has read and accepted the license agreement. On the other hand an application that swallows a SMS and does not display it to the user is a complete malicious activity. There is no justified reason for an application to delete a user designated message even before the message has been displayed to the user or read by the user. The antivirus application does not detect such kind of malicious activity.

A comparison of the computer based antivirus with the Smartphone based antivirus would help to understand why the Smartphone antivirus failed to detect the malicious activity. Computer based antivirus software is signature and anomaly based. Computer based antivirus have certain drivers installed that enable it to get kernel level access such as the Symantec antivirus driver showed in the below picture.

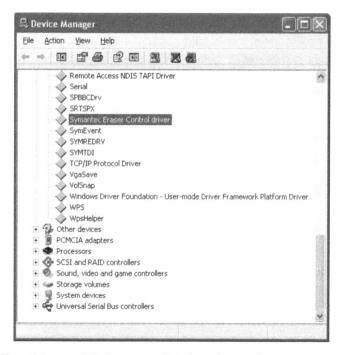

Figure 5 Computer's device manager displaying an installed Symantec driver

As the antivirus has kernel level access, it can look for anomaly based malicious activity such as 'key stroke loggers', perform 'Deep Packet Inspection', look for malicious processes, etc. The computer architecture allows kernel level access to the antivirus software. This enables the antivirus to detect anomaly based malicious activity.

Unlike the computer operating system, Smartphone operating system architecture of iOS and Android does not allow kernel level access to user level applications, unless the phone is jail broken. The antivirus software is also user level software just like other applications which does not get kernel access. Moreover, the iOS and Android's application isolation policy does not allow an application to access information or data of another application. Every application runs in its own sandbox which gives an impression to the application that it is the only one on the phone. The below snippet shows that Symantec mobile security is running in application layer as app_39. Every app is treated as a user and has unique username and access rights assigned to it.

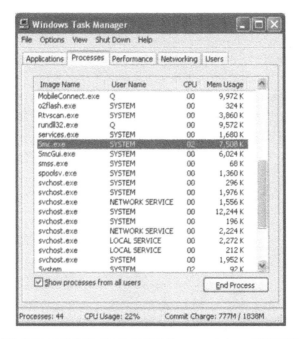

Figure 6 Symantec mobile security is running as user 'app_39' at application layer

Whereas, the below screenshot shows that 'smc.exe' process which is Symantec antivirus for Microsoft Windows has 'SYSTEM' level access.

Figure 7 Task manager displaying Symantec's Smc.exe running as SYSTEM User

Applications running as root have kernel access. The below snippet shows that safebot application is running as root.

Figure 8 Safebot malware is running as root user

Below are the concluding points-

a. Smartphone antivirus does not work in the same way as computer antivirus work.

b. Smartphone antivirus does not have kernel level access to detect root kits.

c. They cannot interact with other processes due to the sandboxing or isolation policies.

d. If a Smartphone application is exploited by a malware, the damage is limited to that specific application, once again due to sandboxing. However, if the operating system is exploited by the malware, it might get kernel access which could cause more damage.

e. Smartphone antivirus products are signature based and not anomaly based.

f. The Smartphone operating system displays a 'User Access control' notification for user level application activity such as sending SMS or other data. It should also display a 'User Access control' notification for applications having root level access. This is because, a malware might exploit operating system vulnerability and gain root access. The operating system should have a tamper resistant list application of access rights for activities such as, sending SMS or access to contacts, emails, etc. The list should be protected in such a way, that it should not be modified by a malware to include its name in the list. Technically, this will help to identify whether the operating system is compromised if it detects an application performing malicious activity. The user could then be notified of the malicious activity.

g. The phone that is purchased from eBay is a used one. It is quite possible that a used phone being sold on eBay might have a Trojan. To be on a safer side, install the latest firmware on the phone before one starts using it. If the phone already has latest firmware, one could flash the ROM and install a fresh copy of the latest firmware.

The next chapter discusses some attacks on Smartphones and possible protective measures.

Chapter 5 Attacks on Smartphones

5.1 Introduction

As the popularity of Smartphone increases the risk associated to it also increase. Thus, it is very important to analyse the various possible attacks and threats to a Smartphone to find various preventative measures. This chapter considers various threats, the source of the threat, the likelihood impact of the threat and the possible protective measures.

5.2 Attacks and threats to Smartphone

Below are some of the attacks and threats to a Smartphone.

5.2.1 Malicious Applications such as, Virus, Malware and Trojan

Malicious applications have been successful to cause damage to computers. Probably, it's the computer architecture that allows applications to get kernel access, interact with other processes and read/write to the disk. However, there are a very few instances of successful exploits by malicious applications for non-jail broken phones. There are a few exploits for jail broken phones but, not in the wild. Even if a malicious application manages to compromise an application, the damage is limited to that application and the data that application uses. As Android is not strict about application signing, there have been some Trojans for Android. Thus it is very important that users are aware what they are installing and the permissions they are granting to the application. One of the favourite Android app of Trojan writers is the 'Angry Birds' app. There have been several versions of this app that are Trojans. Both, Android and iOS have been successful against malware however; Android needs to implement strict signing process for application developers to avoid Trojans. Google remotely wipes Trojans from the phones once it confirms.

Examples of Android and iOS Trojans

Android.Lightdd [50] – Steals user sensitive information from the phone and uploads to malicious websites.

Android.Rootcager [51] – Steals user sensitive information from the phone and uploads to malicious websites.

iPhoneOS.Ikee [52] – Changes the wallper of the iPhone

Below are the comments by a Google spokesman about the effect of the Trojan on Android OS [53].

"Our application permissions model protects against this type of threat. When installing an application, users see a screen that explains clearly what information and system resources the application has permission to access, such as a user's phone number or sending an SMS. Users must explicitly approve this access in order to continue with the installation, and they may uninstall applications at any time. We consistently advise users to only install apps they trust. In particular, users should exercise caution when installing applications outside of Android Market."

Till date, the successful malware exploits were for jail broken phones. Clearly, jail broken phones should not be allowed in enterprises. Administrators should have strict policies and procedures and strong network access control mechanism to check that jail broken phones are not connecting the enterprise's network. Conventional computers use 'Host Integrity' tools that define rules for a computer that wishes to connect to enterprise network. If a computer does not comply with the minimum requirements of software version requirements, it is not allowed to connect to the network and it is put in 'Quarantine' VLAN. The administrator can be notified of these kinds of non-patched machines by the host integrity application so that the machines can be upgraded with required software before connecting to the corporate network. Similarly, a tool like 'Host Integrity' and network access control could help to check the Smartphone for specific version before it connects to the network.

For example: Symantec Endpoint Protection has Host Integrity and Network Access control for enterprise computers.

Source

Trojans and malware can come from sources like Internet, Application store and removable media.

Impact

a. Loss of data such as browsing history, login details, credit card details

b. Loss of money if SMS messages are sent without user intervention to premium numbers.

Protective Measures

a. User should be aware of what they are downloading

b. User should read the 'End User License Agreement' before installing the application.

c. User should know what permissions they are granting to the application and the possible implications.

d. Both Android and iOS should release updates to patch vulnerabilities to keep away malware and remove known Trojans from the app stores immediately.

e. Use antivirus software so that known malware and Trojans are detected.

5.2.2 Vulnerabilities

The attacker manages to exploit vulnerability in an application such as a web browser. The attack is launched by a malicious website or a website that is compromised by a malicious attacker. The server on which these websites are hosted, determine the type of browser and the vulnerabilities. The user's web browser is then infected by the web server. The compromised web browser can execute remote code which allows the attacker to send specially crafted malicious instructions to the user's web browser in such a way, that the user's web browser sends information such as browsing history, login details, credit card details, form data, etc. to the attacker.

Example 1: "Webkit Floating Point Datatype Remote Code Execution Vulnerability" found in various browsers and software [54].

Example 2: "Norton Mobile Security for Android Beta Vulnerability in accessing Android system logs"

A known vulnerability in Norton Mobile Security accesses Android system logs [55].

Source

Vulnerability in applications and operating system can be exploited by malicious websites and malwares.

Impact

Vulnerabilities can result in exploitation by threats that could steal user sensitive data.

Protective Measures

a. Install software updates and operating system updates for the Smartphone regularly.

b. Avoid clicking unknown links as they might contain malicious code.

c. Update web servers regularly to avoid been exploited by other malicious websites and web browsers.

5.2.3 False positive detection

When an antivirus detects a good file as a malicious file, it is regarded as false positive. So far there have been no instances of false positive detections by a Smartphone antivirus. However, one cannot deny the fact that a false positive for Smartphone might not occur.

There have been several instances of false positive detections by signature definitions of computer antivirus products such as McAfee and Norton. For example, a signature release by McAfee antivirus detected svchost.exe which is a critical Microsoft windows file as a malicious file, and deleted it which resulted in system crash. Apparently, there were workarounds to fix the issue by booting the operating system in safe mode or some other way [56].

As an analogy from the computer world, if a Smartphone antivirus detects a false positive which leads to a system crash, it might not be possible for some Smartphone's to fix it without reinstalling the operating system. In such kind of an event, there is potential data loss if the operating system has to be completely reinstalled.

Source

A critical system file deleted by a false positive detection by an antivirus that might crash the operating system of the phone.

Impact

Loss of user data such as files, contacts, emails, etc.

Protective Measures

a. One protective measure that administrators can take is to verify the definitions in test environment if the antivirus signatures are distributed by the enterprise to the end user Smartphone. However there is little to avoid false positive detection if the Smartphone gets update directly from the Internet.

b. As a protective measure, administrators can set the Smartphone to synchronize data.

c. From mass market point of view, users could synchronize their Smartphone with computers to ensure they have their data backed up.

5.2.4 Removable card

Removable cards carry substantial amount of data which might include information like contacts, emails, files, application data, etc. iOS provides full device encryption for iPhone. However, Android does not provide encryption for Smartphone as of now. Android 3.0 for tablets provides encryption for tablets however; Android 3.0 will be released for Smartphones by the end of 2011. Motorola Xoom if the first tablet to have Android 3.0 with encryption supported by Android. If an Android phone is lost or left unattended, a malicious user can connect it to a computer using an USB cable and copy data whereas, iOS protects iPhone from these kind of attacks.

Source

Loss of device and phone left unattended for a long time without encryption for removable cards.

Impact

Data is lost if it is not encrypted.

Protective Measures

a. For iPhone: Ensure a strong password is configured to login to the device as iOS does not allow the data to be accessed in plain text while the phone is locked.

b. For Android: Android 3.0 for phones is expected to be released by the end of 2011. Upgrade the phone to Android 3.0 once it is released to enable full device encryption. Meanwhile, users can use any encryption software that is available in Android market.

c. Administrators for enterprise users can enforce encryption by using tools like *"Kaspersky Endpoint Security for Smartphone* [57]*"*

5.2.5 Loss of device

Mobile phones are small and could be easily lost due to negligence. Often people forget their phones in coffee shops, cinema halls, railways, classrooms, etc.

Source

a. Negligence by end user leads to loss of device.

b. Other factors such as riots, accidents, natural disasters, etc.

Impact

a. Loss of device.

b. Loss of user sensitive data like, contacts, emails, files etc.

Protective Measures

a. Users should take preventive measures to prevent loss of phone.

b. Ensure a strong password is configured to unlock the phone.

c. Administrators can configure the device to wipe itself, after specific failed login attempts.

d. Use encryption to encrypt the data on the phone including the removable card.

e. Mass market users can check with their operator whether they provide remote wipe service. For example, Sprint provides remote wipe service [58]

f. Ensure anti-theft application is installed which might help to track the device.

5.2.6 Social Engineering

Smartphone's have been approved for work by many enterprises and government agencies.

A team of UK government was on an official tour to China in July 2008. Labour minister Gordon Brown, MP of the labour party was a victim of a social engineering attack. It is suspected that it was a crafted 'honey trap' by Chinese intelligence. While the officials were partying in a disco, a beautiful Chinese girl approached Mr Brown; they danced together for some time and disappeared. Next morning, Gordon Brown reported that his phone was missing.

Here's a snippet of the news reported by 'The Times' [59]

"The group stayed at the disco for at least two hours. One senior aide was approached by an attractive Chinese woman. The couple danced and later disappeared together.

The security official said: "In these circumstances it was not wise. Nobody knows exactly what happened after they left. But the next morning he came forward and said: "My BlackBerry is missing." The prime minister's Special Branch protection team was alerted"

Users of social engineering websites like MySpace, Twitter, Facebook, etc. are victims of social engineering attacks. Orkut is a social networking site by Google which displays a list of profile visitors. Facebook does not provide this feature however, Facebook users are curious to know who viewed their profile. Taking advantage of this curiosity, some malicious apps claim to display a list of profile visitors. When the user clicks on the link to check their profile view, the app requests for permissions such as, "Access my basic information", "Post to my wall", "Access my data any time". The user

43

allows the application to access data despite reading the permission requests by the application.

Source

a. Victims of other fraudulent people that tend to be friendly.

b. A socially engineered attack crafted by malicious attacker that uses the latest news or happening events to tempt the users to click on links.

c. User curiosity to know something that tempts them to click on the link.

Impact

a. Loss of data and personal information.

b. Infecting other people in the network or friends list.

c. Creating and spreading spam information unknowingly.

Protective Measures

a. Users should have adequate security measures on their phone to ensure that, data is not lost in case a phone is stolen.

b. User awareness should be created by the owner of the service provider such as Facebook.

c. User should know what links they are clicking.

d. If user feels a link is malicious, user should investigate by using search engines or social media to find out whether the link is malicious before clicking it.

This chapter discussed some attacks on Smartphones and the possible protective measures. The next chapter analyses cloud based security solutions.

Chapter 6 Analysis of cloud based security solutions

This chapter analyses other possible security solutions to minimize the security processing overload from the Smartphone. Smartphone's are small in size and are battery conscious devices. One should know what applications and services the phone is running as the number of services and applications has a direct impact on the battery life of the phone. One reason why computer users might not like antivirus products is they slow down the computer. However, a computer user is not too much worried about the power consumption. On the other hand a Smartphone user is conscious about the battery consumption. An antivirus on the Smartphone can use significant processor cycles and the battery as well. It is also important to use the latest protection information to have effective protection. Cloud security or SaaS (Security as a Service) is an alternative to the conventional security framework where the security check is not performed on the endpoint device. The below picture shows an overview of cloud based security services.

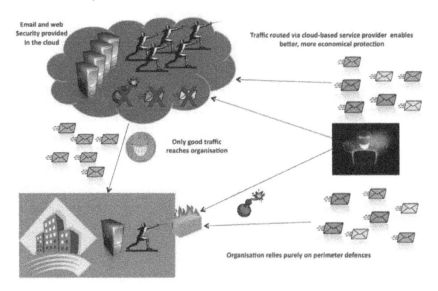

Figure 9 Shows how a cloud-based email and web security service works [60]

The idea is to pass and process all the web and email traffic through the cloud security provider before it reaches the corporate network. The device could be a Smartphone, a roaming laptop or a desktop in the office. Cloud security provides, unified security for devices. It also minimizes the security processing on the endpoint by eliminating unwanted traffic before it reaches the endpoint device. Organizations can sign a Service Level Agreement with the cloud security service provider. The cloud security service provider performs security check as per the norms and the Service Level Agreement set by the organization that buys the service.

There are several vendors that provide cloud security services. This service is for enterprise customers.

Enterprises have several benefits of availing cloud based security service.

a. Email and web content filtering is done by the cloud security service provider before the traffic reaches the enterprise network.
b. Enterprises don't have to buy the hardware to host the security services.
c. Enterprises don't have to have skilled specialist to implement the security services.
d. As the threat landscape changes, the cloud security providers improve the security proactively.

Below are some of the vendors that provide cloud based security services.

a. McAfee
b. Symantec Message labs
c. Cisco ScanSafe
d. Zscaler
e. Websense
f. Panda Security
g. Baracuda Networks

Chapter 7 Conclusion

A computer antivirus focuses on protection against virus, Trojan, malware, root kits and web browsing whereas, a Smartphone antivirus focuses of features like antivirus, Anti-theft , GPS tracking and remote wipe. I feel that there are two more components that should be included in a Smartphone antivirus. Some Smartphone antivirus products provide these features however, it is not found in most of them. The features are-

a. **Backup:** Antivirus should backup data like contacts and files. Whenever a phone is lost, users can restore data like contacts to a new phone.

b. **Application Auditing:** Application auditing maintains the details of application activity and permission request of all the applications. A common behaviour found in most of the computer and Smartphone users is, installing applications without reading the 'End User License Agreement'. One reason could be a psychological trend set by 'End User License Agreement' of computer software. The 'End User License Agreement' of computer software is too long and the language used in most of them is legal, which most of the common users fail to understand. Users click on "I Accept" button without reading it and install the software. Users have the same 'End User License Agreement' mind set for Smartphone software as well. The irony is, even though the 'Permission request' screen lists the permissions in a short and simple manner that is understood by common user, users don't seem to read it before installing the application. This might lead in installing a Trojan application that sends SMS to premium rate numbers and ends up the user in high bills at the end of the month. Another implication is that the application might steal user sensitive information like browsing history, passwords, contacts, etc., which leads to identity theft. If the user comes across such kind of suspicious behaviour there should be a way to find out a summary of activity and permissions of the installed applications. The user can go ahead and uninstall applications to which they have granted unwanted permission.

Android and iOS platforms implement access control to access the device and also have options to wipe the device after certain failed login attempts. Both the platforms implement sandboxing for application isolation. Apple provides full device encryption, whereas Android has not yet implemented encryption for Smartphones. Android 3.0 has started supporting encryption for tablets starting with Motorola Xoom. Android 3.0 for Smartphones will be released by the end of 2011. Both the platforms implement permission based access control so that applications request the user to grant the permission to access the resources. Both the platforms implement application signing to track back the authors in case a malicious application is discovered. Apple's signing process and application certification is very rigorous which prevents Trojan app developers away as they will be prosecuted if they are found guilty. On the other hand, Google's application signing process is not rigorous. Google charges $25 fee for registration which is paid by credit card. The Credit card is only the way to bind the identity of the developer to the application. However, a malicious developer who has details of someone else's credit card can create fake certificates and upload Trojan apps in the market. This is one reason why there are so many Trojan apps for Android. Google should strengthen their application signing model to reduce Trojan apps.

A proof of Concept malware that has root access of an Android phone, can intercept user SMS messages. An antivirus running at the application layer cannot detect this kind of kernel level activity. In other words, Smartphone antivirus cannot detect root kits.

Enterprise antivirus products for mobile Management should include support for all the mobile platforms. This would enable enterprises to allow employees to use the Smartphone of their choice at the same time; the enterprise could enforce policies for the phones. Apart from the features of the mass market Smartphone antivirus, two important components that an enterprise Mobile management solution should have is, *Encryption* and *Host Integrity & Network Access Control*. Enterprises should not allow use of jail broken phones to connect to corporate networks for work.

Future Work

The practical work involved in this project uses a HTC G1 Android phone. Similar kind of Proof of Concept practical work can be carried out on iPhone or Windows Mobile as well. The project does not concentrate on Smartphone security for enterprise related to Microsoft Exchange or Lotus notes. Another area of research is to find out whether as antivirus application can be developed to get root access to detect kernel level malicious activity.

References

[1] Susan Hansche, John Berti, Chris Hare, Official (ISC) [2] Guide to CISSP Exam, Auerbach Publications, 2004, Page number 819

[2] Susan Hansche, John Berti, Chris Hare, Official (ISC) [2] Guide to CISSP Exam, Auerbach Publications, 2004, Page number 231

[3] Peter Szor, The Art of Computer Virus Research and Defense, 2005, Page 36

[4] Susan Hansche, John Berti, Chris Hare, Official (ISC) [2] Guide to CISSP Exam, Auerbach Publications, 2004, Page number 301

[5] Symantec Whitepaper, Symantec Endpoint Protection - A unified, proactive approach to endpoint security, July 2011,
http://webobjects.cdw.com/webobjects/media/pdf/symantec/Endpoint-Security-Whitepaper.pdf
Page number 8

[6] Symantec Whitepaper, Symantec Endpoint Protection A unified, proactive approach to endpoint security, July 2011,
http://webobjects.cdw.com/webobjects/media/pdf/symantec/Endpoint-Security-Whitepaper.pdf
Page number 13

[7] Susan Hansche, John Berti, Chris Hare, Official (ISC) [2] Guide to CISSP Exam, Auerbach Publications, 2004, Page 206

[8] Susan Hansche, John Berti, Chris Hare, Official (ISC) [2] Guide to CISSP Exam, Auerbach Publications, 2004, Page 595-596

[9] Symantec Administration guide, Symantec Network Access Control Policy Manager Administration Guide 5.1, December 2005
ftp://ftp.symantec.com/public/english_us_canada/products/symantec_network_access_control/5.1/manuals/SNAC_5_1_Policy_Manager_Administration_Guide.pdf Page number 4

[10] McAfee Whitepaper, Proactive Threat Protection: Reducing the "Window of Vulnerability",
Aug 2011, http://www.crswann.com/2-NetSecurity/ProactiveThreatProtection%28McAfee%29.pdf Page 4

[11] McAfee Whitepaper, Proactive Threat Protection: Reducing the "Window of Vulnerability",
Aug 2011, http://www.crswann.com/2-NetSecurity/ProactiveThreatProtection%28McAfee%29.pdf Page 7

[12] Symantec Whitepaper, Symantec Endpoint Protection A unified, proactive approach to endpoint security, July 2011, http://webobjects.cdw.com/webobjects/media/pdf/symantec/Endpoint-Security-Whitepaper.pdf Page number 14

[13] Norton, Norton 360 Version 5,0 Premier Edition http://us.norton.com/360-premier-edition/ Aug 2011

[14] McAfee, McAfee Total Protection 2011, http://home.mcafee.com/Store/PackageDetail.aspx?pkgid=275 Aug 2011

[15] Kaspersky, Internet Security Special Ferrari Edition, http://www.kaspersky.co.uk/kaspersky-internet-security-special-ferrari-edition?blocknum2=2 Aug 2011

[16] Webroot, Webroot Mobile Security for Android, http://www.webroot.com/En_US/consumer-products-mobile-security-android-phone.html Aug 2011

[17] Kaspersky user guide, Kaspersky Mobile Security 9.0, http://www.it2trust.com/pdf/Kaspersky.Mobile.Security.9.0.EN.pdf Aug 2011 Page number 7

[18] Kaspersky user guide, Kaspersky Mobile Security 9.0, http://www.it2trust.com/pdf/Kaspersky.Mobile.Security.9.0.EN.pdf Aug 2011 Page number 7

[19] McAfee, McAfee Mobile Security, https://www.mcafeemobilesecurity.com/default.aspx Aug 2011

[20] Kaspersky user guide, Kaspersky Mobile Security 9.0, http://www.it2trust.com/pdf/Kaspersky.Mobile.Security.9.0.EN.pdf Aug 2011 Page number 7

[21] Webroot, Webroot Mobile Security for Android, http://www.webroot.com/En_US/consumer-products-mobile-security-android-phone.html Aug 2011

[22] Norton, Norton mobile security, http://us.norton.com/mobile-security/ Aug 2011

[23] Kasperskt, Kaspersky mobile Security, http://www.kaspersky.co.uk/kmsppc?&THRU=&thru=reseller%3DSEM_43103%26mcky%3D mkwid|s1awCZiOA|pcrid|7040487203|plid||kword|kapersky%2520mobile%26gclid%3DCJaSuK bx8aoCFdQNfAodsVCWlg Aug 2011

[24] Webroot, Webroot for mobile security, http://www.webroot.com/En_US/consumer-products-mobile-security-Android-phone.html Aug 2011

[25] McAfee, Macafee Mobile Security, https://www.mcafeemobilesecurity.com/default.aspx Aug 2011

[26] Bitdefender, Bitdefender Mobile Security, http://m.bitdefender.com/features.html Aug 2011

[27] BullGuard, BullGuard Mobile Security, http://www.bullguard.com/why/bullguard-mobile-security-10.aspx Aug 2011

[28] Trend Micro, Trend Micro Security for Android, http://us.trendmicro.com/us/products/personal/titanium-maximum-security/index.html?tabCont0=3 Aug 2011

[29] Lookout, Lookout Mobile Security, https://www.mylookout.com/features/management 2011 Aug 2011

[30] Whitepaper by context information Security LTD – "Smartphones in the Enterprise", http://www.contextis.co.uk/resources/white-papers/smartphones/Context-Smartphone-White_Paper.pdf 13th December 2010

[31] Symantec, Symantec Mobile Management for Enterprise, http://www.symantec.com/en/uk/business/theme.jsp?themeid=mobile-security-management Aug 2011

[32] Kaspersky, Kaspersky Endpoint Security for Smartphone, http://www.kaspersky.co.uk/kaspersky-endpoint-security-smartphone Aug 2011

[33] McAfee, McAfee Enterprise Mobility Management (McAfee EMM), http://www.mcafee.com/us/products/enterprise-mobility-management.aspx Aug 2011

[34] Carey Nachenberg, Whitepaper by Symantec – "A Window Into Mobile Device Security", http://www.symantec.com/content/en/us/about/media/pdfs/symc_mobile_device_security_june2011.pdf Aug 2011

[35] Apple, iOS Developer Enterprise Program, http://developer.apple.com/support/ios/enterprise.html Aug 2011

[36] CRN, Jail broken iPhones fall victim to Australian virus, http://www.crn.com.au/News/160078,jailbroken-iphones-fall-victim-to-australian-virus.aspx 9 Nov 2009

[37] YouTube, Blackhat conference presenter explains an iPhone attack, http://www.youtube.com/watch?v=bKtTyyViVN8#t=1m17s Aug 2011

[38] Android Developers, Android 3.0 Platform Highlights,
http://developer.Android.com/sdk/Android-3.0-highlights.html Aug 2011

[39] YouTube, How To Root Your T-Mobile G1 with Android 1.6 pt. 1,
http://www.youtube.com/watch?v=u8F7FVISb7w Aug 2011

[40] YouTube, How To Root Your T-Mobile G1 with Android 1.6 pt. 2,
http://www.youtube.com/watch?v=H00kN2K2Q_8 Aug 2011

[41] File download link for RC7,
http://api.viglink.com/api/click?format=go&drKey=1359&loc=http%3A%2F%2Fforum.xda-
developers.com%2Fshowthread.php%3Ft%3D442480&v=1&libid=1313680148910&out=http%
3A%2F%2Fkoushikdutta.blurryfox.com%2FG1%2FDREAMIMG-
RC7.zip&ref=http%3A%2F%2Fwww.google.co.uk%2Fsearch%3Faq%3Df%26sourceid%3Dchr
ome%26ie%3DUTF-8%26q%3Dhow%2Bto%2Broot%2Bg1&title=How-to-
%20Root%2C%20Hack%2C%20and%20Flashing%20your%20G1%2FDream%20Read%20first
!!%20-%20xda-developers&txt=RC7&jsonp=vglnk_jsonp_13136801531201 Aug 2011

[42] File download link for signed-kila-ota-148830.de6a94ca.zip, http://Android-
roms.googlecode.com/files/signed-kila-ota-148830.de6a94ca.zip Aug 2011

[43] File download link for flashrec.apk,
http://www.4shared.com/account/file/196526014/ae11f215/flashrec.html Aug 2011

[44] File download link for recovery-RA-dream-v1.5.2.img, http://www.filecrop.com/recovery-
RA-dream-v1.5.2.img.html Aug 2011

[45] File download link for haykuro_new_spl-signed.zip, http://code.google.com/p/Android-
roms/downloads/detail?name=haykuro_new_spl-signed.zip&can=2&q Aug 2011

[46] File download link for signed-dream_devphone_userdebug-ota-14721.zip,
http://www.4shared.com/get/adm_7JS8/signed-dream_devphone_userdebu.html Aug 2011

[47] File download link for update-cm-4.2.13-signed.zip, http://code.google.com/p/cyanogen-
updater/downloads/detail?name=update-cm-4.2.13-signed.zip&can=2&q= Aug 2011

[48] Georgia Weidman's website that provides the download link for 'Proof of Concept' safebot
malware, http://www.grmn00bs.com/2011/07/11/more-Android-sms-bot-stuff Aug 2011

[49] BrightTalk, Georgia Weidman's webinar on "Transparent Botnet Command and Control for
Smartphones over SMS", http://www.brighttalk.com/webcast/574/26197 Aug 2011

[50] Symantec, Details of Android.Lightdd Trojan,
http://www.symantec.com/security_response/writeup.jsp?docid=2011-053114-2342-99 Aug
2011

[51] Symantec, Details of Android.Rootcager Trojan,
http://www.symantec.com/security_response/writeup.jsp?docid=2011-030212-1438-99 Aug
2011

[52] Symantec, Details of iPhoneOS.Ikee worm,
http://www.symantec.com/security_response/writeup.jsp?docid=2009-111015-5423-99 Aug
2011

[53] BBC News, "Virus writers hit Google Android phones",
http://www.bbc.co.uk/news/technology-10928070 11 Aug 2010

[54] Symantec, Webkit Floating Point Datatype Remote Code Execution Vulnerability,
http://www.symantec.com/security_response/vulnerability.jsp?bid=43047 Aug 2011

[55] Norton, Norton Mobile Security for Android Beta Vulnerability in accessing Android
system logs,
http://us.norton.com/support/kb/web_view.jsp?wv_type=public_web&docurl=20101116132826
EN&ln=en_US 4 June 2011

[56] Microsoft, McAfee delivers a false-positive detection of the W32/wecorl.a virus when
version 5958 of the DAT file is used, http://support.microsoft.com/kb/2025695 15 June 2010

[57] Kaspersky, Kaspersky Endpoint Security for Smartphone,
http://www.kaspersky.co.uk/endpoint-security-smartphone Aug 2011

[58] Sprint, Sprint Remote Wipe,
http://sprint.tekgroupweb.com/article_display.cfm?article_id=1948#_highlight&id16=remote+
wipe 15 June 2011

[59] The Times, Gordon Brown aide a victim of honeytrap operation by Chinese agents,
http://www.timesonline.co.uk/tol/news/politics/article4364353.ece July 20 2008

[60] Fran Howarth, A White Paper by Bloor Research - "When the cloud improves security...
move protection to where the threats are",
http://www.webroot.com/shared/pdf/whenthecloudimprovessecurity_BloorResearch_201007140
25943.pdf June 2010